DANGEROUS JOBS

STUNT PERFORMER

BY NICK GORDON

BELLWETHER MEDIA · MINNEAPOLIS, MN

TM

Are you ready to take it to the extreme?
Torque books thrust you into the action-packed world
of sports, vehicles, mystery, and adventure. These books
may include dirt, smoke, fire, and dangerous stunts.
WARNING: read at your own risk.

Library of Congress Cataloging-in-Publication Data

Gordon, Nick.
  Stunt performer / by Nick Gordon.
    pages cm. -- (Torque: dangerous jobs)
  Includes bibliographical references and index.
  Summary: "Engaging images accompany information about stunt performers. The combination
  of high-interest subject matter and light text is intended for students in grades 3 through 7"
  -- Provided by publisher.
  ISBN 978-1-60014-897-2 (hardcover : alk. paper)
  1. Stunt performers--Juvenile literature. I. Title.
  PN1995.9.S7G67 2013
  791.4302'8092--dc23
                              2012041593

This edition first published in 2013 by Bellwether Media, Inc.

Printed in the United States of America, North Mankato, MN.

TABLE OF CONTENTS

CHAPTER 1
ACTION!

It is time to film the movie's big action scene. Two helicopters chase each other in the air. Explosions light up the surrounding sky. Expert pilots bring the helicopters close. The most dangerous **stunt** of the movie is about to begin.

A stunt performer moves to the edge of one helicopter's door. He is dressed to look like one of the actors in the film. The stunt performer leaps out of the helicopter to escape gunfire. Then a fiery explosion erupts as he lands safely on the ground. The stunt worked perfectly. "Cut!" shouts the movie **director**.

The Second Unit

Stunt performers usually work with a film's second unit. This unit focuses on stunts and action scenes. It has its own special director.

CHAPTER 2

STUNT PERFORMERS

Many films and TV shows feature exciting stunts. Movie characters fight, get into car chases, and hang from flying helicopters. Few actors are trained to perform these dangerous stunts. That is where stunt performers come in.

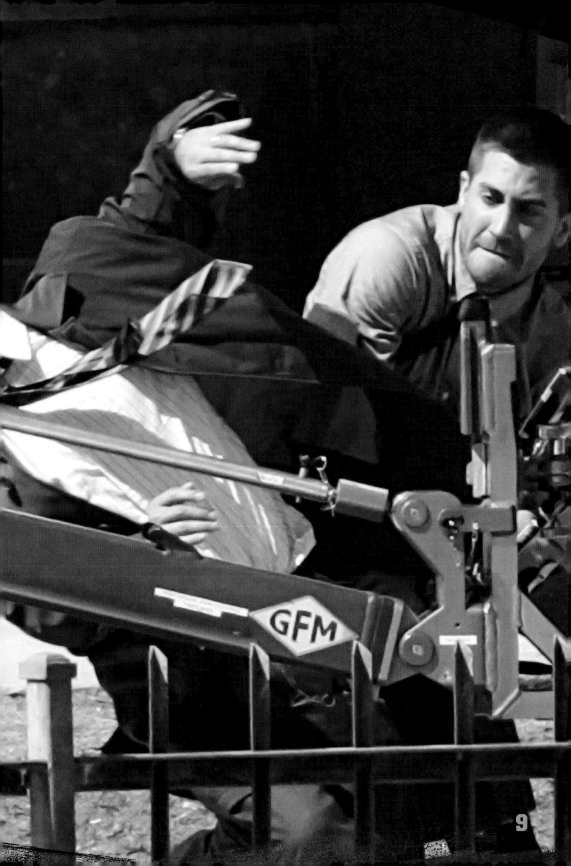

9

Martial Artists

Many stunt performers study martial arts. This training helps them perform fight scenes. It also teaches them excellent body control.

Stunt performers have the skills needed to perform stunts. They are trained to protect their bodies during falls. They learn how to throw punches and kicks that look real but never make contact.

Practice is key to keeping stunt performers safe. Performers **rehearse** every movement they must make. A fight scene that lasts 10 seconds may take days of rehearsal.

Stunt performers also depend on safety gear. They usually fall onto **air bags**. They load guns with **dummy bullets** or **blanks**. Vehicles used in action scenes have a protective **roll cage**.

air bag

Squib It

Stunt performers use tiny explosives called squibs to fake the look of gunshots. They attach the squibs to their bodies. Then they set them off to rip through clothing and burst bags of fake blood.

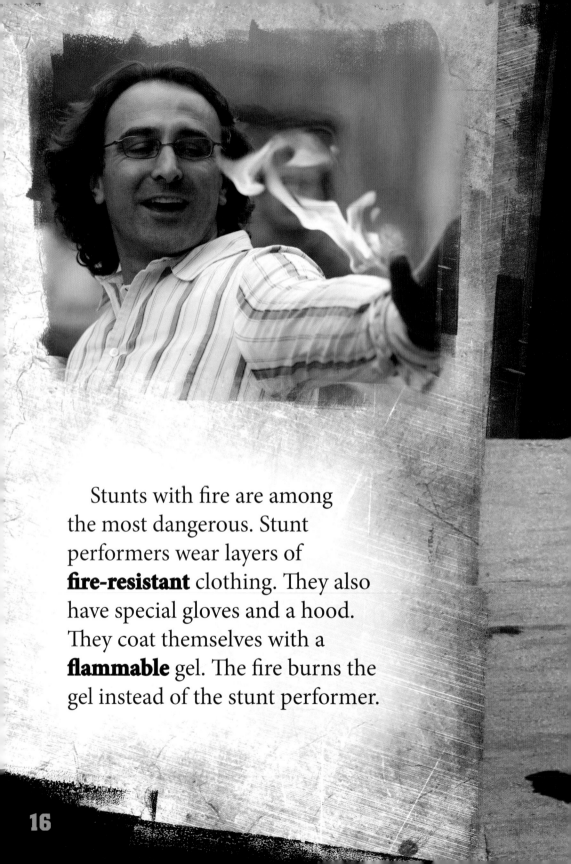

Stunts with fire are among the most dangerous. Stunt performers wear layers of **fire-resistant** clothing. They also have special gloves and a hood. They coat themselves with a **flammable** gel. The fire burns the gel instead of the stunt performer.

CHAPTER 3

DANGER!

Stunt performers do all they can to stay safe. Still, many stunts can injure or even kill. Unexpected crashes can happen. Explosions or fires can get out of control. Stunt performers can miss their targets when they fall.

19

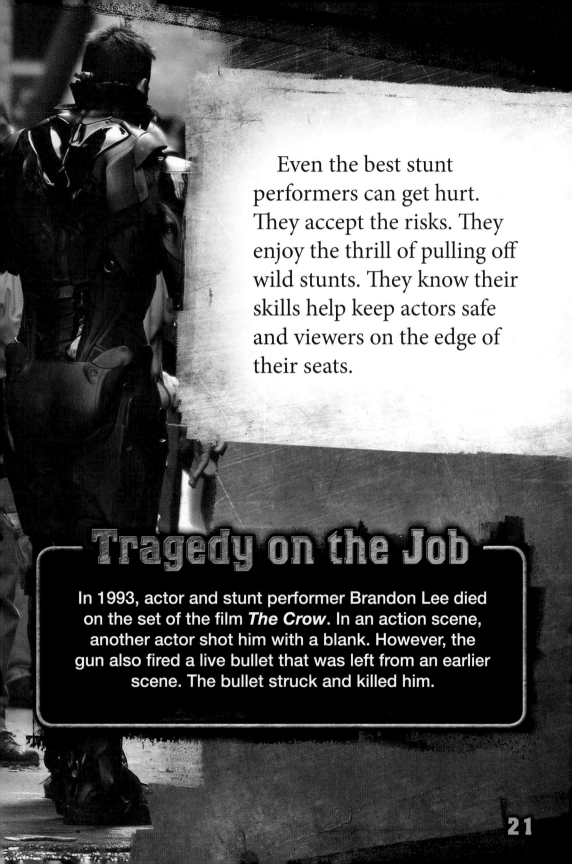

Even the best stunt performers can get hurt. They accept the risks. They enjoy the thrill of pulling off wild stunts. They know their skills help keep actors safe and viewers on the edge of their seats.

Tragedy on the Job

In 1993, actor and stunt performer Brandon Lee died on the set of the film *The Crow*. In an action scene, another actor shot him with a blank. However, the gun also fired a live bullet that was left from an earlier scene. The bullet struck and killed him.

Glossary

air bags—large targets filled with air that cushion stunt performers who do falls

blanks—cartridges for guns that include gunpowder but no bullet; a blank makes noise and a flash.

director—the person in charge of making a movie

dummy bullets—bullets without gunpowder

fire-resistant—difficult to burn

flammable—capable of being set on fire easily

rehearse—to practice a performance

roll cage—metal bars that surround a person inside a vehicle; a roll cage prevents a stunt performer from being crushed during a crash or rollover.

stunt—a difficult or dangerous feat